THE JOSEPH STORY

A Play in Two Acts
(adapted from the *Book of Genesis*)

Rolf McEwen

Wasteland Press
Shelbyville, KY USA
www.wastelandpress.net

The Joseph Story
by Rolf McEwen

Copyright © 2009 Rolf McEwen
ALL RIGHTS RESERVED

First Printing—November 2009
ISBN: 978-1-60047-372-2

Printed in the U.S.A.

CHARACTERS

20 men, 10 women

JACOB, also called ISRAEL, patriarch of the Hebrew family which was heir to God's promises which were made to Abraham, father of the faith

LEAH, Jacob's first wife
ZILPAH, Leah's servant-girl
BILHAH, Rachel's servant-girl

The sons of JACOB--

By LEAH:
REUBEN, the oldest
SIMEON
LEVI
JUDAH
ISSACHAR
ZEBULUN

By RACHEL:
JOSEPH
BENJAMIN

By BILHAH, RACHEL's servant girl:
DAN
NAPHTALI

By ZILPAH, LEAH's servant-girl--
GAD
ASHER

PHARAOH, King of Egypt
WINE TASTER for Pharaoh
BAKER for Pharaoh
POTIPHAR, captain of the palace guard, and chief executioner
POTIPHAR's WIFE
FIRST WISE MAN
SECOND WISE MAN
FIRST MAGICIAN
SECOND MAGICIAN
HOUSE MANAGER to Joseph
CLERK to Joseph
EGYPTIAN COMMONER
CHIEF ISHMAELITE TRADER
ISHMAELITE TRADERS (4)
SOLDIERS (8)
FEMALE SERVANTS (6)
MESSENGER
STRANGER in the land of Shechem

TIME: *2000 B.C., time of the biblical Patriarchs*
PLACE: *The lands of Canaan and Egypt*

Production Note

The play is performed in two acts. Act I runs about 65 minutes and Act II about 55 minutes. Because the action of the play occurs in many locations, it is performed on a bare stage with minimal furniture and props brought on by the actors to enhance each scene. The action of the play is continuous and fluid despite the changes of scenes. Lights do not dim between scenes. Jacob's house can be represented by use of two tables, a bench, and several wooden chairs. The lands of Shechem and Dothan can be represented with a few large rocks and small trees scattered about the stage. Potiphar's house in Egypt should include some simple furnishings typical of the time, including a couch or thick white sheepskin for the scene with Potiphar's wife. Pharaoh's palace includes several tables with food and wine for the celebration, and an extravagant chair suitable for a king. The prison includes some wooden stools, boards for a bed, and a small table.

Thus each setting is represented with simple furnishings that can be moved on and off quickly without delaying the action of the play. Exits are left and right. As actors from one scene exit to one side, actors for the next scene enter from the other, bringing their props and furniture with them. Characters who perform in two consecutive scenes should start to exit with others, then move across stage to join actors who are entering for the ensuing scene. The intent is to progress with the story without wasting time doing complicated scene changes.

NOTE TO PRODUCERS: No payment of royalty is required to produce this play if a sufficient number of scripts is purchased. Producers must purchase copies of the script for every performer, whether or not the play is presented with a fee for admission. Thus, permission is granted to perform *The Joseph Story* without payment of royalty when 30 copies or more of the script are purchased.

SYNOPSIS OF SCENES

ACT I. Jacob's home in the land of Canaan, the land of Shechem, the land of Dothan, and other locations.

ACT II. Jacob's home in the land of Canaan; Potiphar's house; a prison in Egypt; the palace of Pharaoh, King of Egypt; the land of Egypt.

ACT I, SCENE I

SCENE: *JACOB'S house in the land of Canaan. There is a wooden table covered with papers at center stage, another wooden table UR. Several wooden chairs are scattered about the stage, and there is a wooden bench DL. JOSEPH and his brothers enter from doors at right and left, filling the stage, striking up conversation and laughter as they come on. They are dressed in simple long tops tied at the waist, typical of shepherd's clothing of the patriarchal times. They wear sandals. They are rugged men accustomed to the out-of-doors.*

JOSEPH. I had a dream. It was amazing. We were all out in the field binding sheaves, and my sheaf stood up, and all your sheaves gathered around it and bowed down before it!

SIMEON. *(sarcastically)* As usual, everybody bows down to Joseph!

GAD. That's the sort of dream we'd *expect* you to have, Joseph--one that puts you as our master.

JUDAH. Is it too much for you to accept that you're just about the youngest of all of us, Little Great One? Must you always lord it over us in your dreams? Father gives you a fancy coat-of-many-colors, and suddenly you think you're God's gift to the world!

JOSEPH. *(defensively)* Is it my fault that father gave me a beautiful coat? You're all envious because I got something that you didn't. If you weren't so jealous maybe God would give you something nice too.

LEVI. In your dreams you're always our master! *You have far more pleasant dreams about yourself than I have about you*, I'll tell you that! You're a punk, Joseph! Last week I dreamt you were eaten by a bear on your way to the synagogue. *(laughter and backslapping)*

JOSEPH. I don't invent my dreams. They come from God. And for your information, I had another dream a few nights ago. This time the sun, the moon, and eleven stars bowed down to me.

JUDAH. You're out of your mind! The sun and moon bowed down to you? Who do you think you are?

SIMEON. *(bowing low in mockery with his face to the ground)* O Mighty Joseph, may I wipe the dust from your sandals?

ISSACHAR. *(bowing low to the ground)* Mighty One, allow me to carry your sling and bow! May I bring you something to drink?

(JACOB enters R.)

JACOB. Hello, my sons.

SIMEON. Father, Joseph is telling us about more of his silly dreams. He had one in which all of *our* sheaves bowed down to *his*. He had another dream in which the sun, the moon, and stars bowed before him!

(The brothers laugh loudly.)

JUDAH. For a seventeen year old, he thinks much too highly of himself, father. Nobody can accuse him of lacking confidence. This boy's problem is *pride*.

GAD. I think he's trying to compensate for a deeply rooted inferiority complex.

ISSACHAR. Being so very young and weak can cause a fellow to fear the superior knowledge and experience of more mature men!

JACOB. Joseph, no more stories about your dreams! What? Shall I and your mother and your brothers bow before you? Let me hear no more of it.

ASHER. He's always boasting about himself. He thinks he's better than the rest of us. He's too good for us.

DAN. His nose sticks up so high he has to kneel to pass through the city gates! His nose *is* pretty long, but he doesn't have to carry it straight up!

GAD. It's a burden to lift such an enormous thing so high!

(laughter and backslapping)

JACOB. Boys, quit quarreling and find something useful to do. No more foolishness. I don't want to hear any more talk about dreams, you hear me? I don't have time for squabbles over who will bow down to whom. Joseph, I need to talk with you. Come with me.

(They exit together R.)

SIMEON. There goes father and his favorite son. We should buy them matching coats for the next Festival of Colors.

REUBEN. O Simeon, forget about it, even if his dreams *are* ridiculous. And insulting.

(There are nods of agreement, some shaking their heads in disbelief.)

ACT I, SCENE II

SCENE: *JACOB is at home sitting at a desk where he is writing and doing some business. His wife LEAH is in the room. LEAH is sewing a shirt, while BILHAH, the former servant of JACOB'S first wife RACHEL, is helping make loaves of bread. LEAH'S servant ZILPAH is sweeping the floor. It is a domestic scene of household chores.*

JACOB. God has been good to us this month. We have had twenty lambs born in ten days, and we have made profitable trades with our wool.

LEAH. Can I buy fabric for some new gowns, Jacob? I'm tired of my old things. Always the same stuff.

BILHAH. You promised us new bracelets and earrings, Jacob.

LEAH. I want some gold anklets from Egypt.

BILHAH. And I want silk to make nightgowns. You don't want us sleeping another year in these worn-out old nightgowns!

LEAH. O, do *you* sleep in those old things, Bilhah? *I* don't. He gave me something more exciting than that! Jacob honey, didn't you get Bilhah any new nightgowns like the ones you bought for me? The nice *sheer* ones? O, too bad, Bilhah.

BILHAH. Viper! He didn't get you anything new. You should see what he's done for me, *secretly*.

JACOB. Ladies, *please*! I'll buy you both nice new things, just what you like. But no more bickering! Shalom, shalom.

LEAH. You would have had *shalom* if you had been content with *one* wife instead of *two*.

BILHAH.   Not to mention your two concubines. Remember, Leah, if Jacob had chosen only *one* wife, it wouldn't have been *you*. Rachel was the one.

LEAH. Quite a surprise for all of us, wasn't it! *(she smirks)*

BILHAH. It's not every man who loves a woman enough to work fourteen years to get her! How long did he work for you, Leah?

LEAH. I was the *preferred* gift to my husband, selected by father as the first and best bride granted to a very lucky man.

BILHAH. It must be a shock for a man to experience a wedding ceremony with *one* woman and awake in the morning with *another*!

(She glances at the ladies, and then at JACOB.)

JACOB. I can't begin to tell you how surprised I was. That was the last time I slept in the dark. And I cut back on the wine. Now, girls, no more squabbling.

BILHAH. I never have been able to figure out how a man and woman can spend their first night together in the marriage bed without discovering who they are really with.

LEAH. We didn't do any *talking*.

JACOB. Stop right there. Enough! I'm touched by your concern, Bilhah, but let's not cry over spilled milk. It was a wedding. Lots of food and drink.

ZILPAH. Jacob, should Leah's servant be despised for bearing Jacob two sons? Yes, I too have labored for the man of the house! *(she smiles sweetly)* I think you should send some gifts to me, don't you?

JACOB. Yes, yes, I love you all. All are wonderful, and I thank you for bearing me many sons.

LEAH. But I am your *favorite*, aren't I, Jacob?

BILHAH. Go admire your figure in a mirror, gorgeous.
  And get yourself a face-lift.
JACOB. Please! Let's be friends.
LEAH. Friends! You call us friends? I hope you don't
  treat all your friends like you treat us!
JACOB. Leah, do me a favor, will you? Run out and tell
  Joseph to come see me.
BILHAH. Yes, Leah. Run along now.
LEAH. I'm not going anywhere. You'll sidle up to him
  and coax money out of him when I'm gone.
ZILPAH. O, *I'll* go find Joseph.
JACOB. Never mind, Zilpah. I'll go myself. I'm tired of
  the fussing and fighting. Fresh air and silence will be a
  blessing.
(JACOB exits R.)
ZILPAH. *(addressing LEAH and BILHAH)* Must we
  keep this up forever? Can't we forgive and forget?
BILHAH. Easy for *you* to say--this is *your* week to sleep
  in his bed. But let's live and let live--share and share
  alike.
LEAH. We've done that well enough! Yes, Zilpah, you're
  right. I'm sorry.
BILHAH. *(looking ashamed)* I'm sorry too.
(JACOB and JOSEPH enter from stage right, talking.)
JACOB. Your brothers are in Shechem grazing the flocks.
  Go see how they're getting along, and how the flocks
  are doing, and bring me the news.
JOSEPH. I will. Can I leave in the morning? It's a long
  trip.
JACOB. Yes. Be careful, my son. It's not safe to travel
  alone. God be with you.

ACT I, SCENE III

SCENE: *The land of Shechem. Some large rocks are scattered about the stage. JOSEPH is in search of his brothers. He carries a bundle over his shoulder, including food and a blanket. He walks toward a stranger who is tying some things together.*

STRANGER. *(seeing JOSEPH)* Greetings, friend. Where are you going?

JOSEPH. *(setting down his bundle)* I'm looking for my brothers. They're grazing their flocks in this area. Have you seen them?

STRANGER. Yes, but they're no longer here. I heard them say they were going to Dothan.

JOSEPH. Wouldn't you know it? I walk for two days to Shechem, and then they've moved to Dothan!

STRANGER. Isn't that the way it goes? Well, don't let it ruin your day. How about a cold drink? Sit down and rest yourself. *(He lifts a bag of water and hands it to JOSEPH.)* This will refresh you.

JOSEPH. Thank you. *(takes a long, deep drink)* Ah, so cold! You must have drawn from a deep well!

STRANGER. Yes! God has given me a deep well. The LORD be praised.

JOSEPH. Amen.

<h1 style="text-align:center">ACT I, SCENE IV</h1>

SCENE: *The land of Dothan. Trees and rocks are scattered about. JOSEPH'S brothers are sitting around relaxing. They are eating pomegranates, dates, raisins, figs, as well as drinking water.*

ASHER. *(staring at the horizon, squinting)* Someone is coming. Look out there. *(He points as everybody looks.)*

GAD. I think it's that worthless brother of ours. *(straining to see clearly, pausing)* Yes, I think it's Joseph!

SIMEON. He's come to tell us some more of his silly dreams! I suppose he'll say even the LORD himself has bowed before him this time!

ASHER. The arrogant fool! Let's kill him and toss him in a well and tell father a wild animal has eaten him. Then we'll see what becomes of his dreams!

JUDAH. It's what he deserves, the fool.

REUBEN. No, we'd better not kill him. We shouldn't shed the blood of our own brother. Let's throw him into that well over there. *(pointing)* That way he'll die without our doing it directly. We don't want his blood on our hands.

JUDAH. Right. Let's throw him in the well and let him die of natural causes.

GAD. It's a good idea. It'll just so happen that Joseph takes in too much water. What do you say? *(He looks at the others. They look at one another, some nodding, others considering.)*

ASHER. *(motioning for everybody to come to him)* Let's make a pact. Join hands, and we'll see that he gets what he deserves. *(they clasp hands)* All together now: "Down with the dreamer!" Say it twice.

BROTHERS *(swearing together).* "Down with the dreamer, down with the dreamer!"

ASHER. When he gets here, let's give him some food and drink. Then when he's resting, we'll jump him throw him down the well. Okay?

BROTHERS. *(agreeing)* Okay!

(Brothers sit for awhile until JOSEPH enters UL carrying his bundle.)

JOSEPH. So here you are! I've been searching all over the country for you. May I beg a bite to eat? Father sent me to see how things are going.

JUDAH. Joseph, good to see you. Come here and sit down. How did you find us?

JOSEPH. I saw a man in Shechem who said you were moving on to Dothan. It's a long journey, but it was good to see the countryside! I had lots of time alone with God, to walk and talk with no distractions.

REUBEN. Have you had any more dreams, Joseph?

JOSEPH. No new dreams. Hey guys, I'm sorry I troubled you with the others. Have you forgiven me?

ASHER. Forgiven you, Joseph? No, I don't believe we have.

(He stands and walks behind JOSEPH, motioning to the others, who begin to rise.)

JOSEPH. I didn't think telling you my dreams would make you so angry.

GAD. You better think more carefully next time. Think before you make your older brothers out to be inferior to you. We don't appreciate it. *(He falls upon JOSEPH and holds him. All the brothers shout and fall upon him. They pull off his brightly-covered robe and drag him away to the well off-stage, where they*

toss him down. GAD speaks in a loud voice.) Now
you'll have plenty of time to dream. Dream in the dark
where there are no distractions, not even the clouds
and sun! Dream about crawling up the sides of a
twenty-foot well!

ASHER. *(shouting)* You can boast about it. I will bow to
your greatness then!

JUDAH. *(shouting and mocking)* Too bad it's a dry well,
Joseph. You could have something to drink and do
some swimming in the dark.

SIMEON. Count your blessings, Joseph! Be thankful you
don't have to tread water. Your well has just run dry,
little brother! *(laughter and hand-motions by
SIMEON as if he is treading water, moving his hands
across the surface)*

GAD. *(finding a comfortable place to sit)* Now we can
eat in peace, and enjoy a meal without thinking about
that punk! Pass the figs and raisins. Father's favorite
can now enjoy his dreams alone.

(Everybody smiles and passes food around.)

REUBEN. I'll see you boys later. I've got business to
attend to.

(REUBEN exits L.)

SIMEON. I'll bet Joseph will have some incredible dreams
tonight. He can certainly commune with God without
distraction.

JUDAH. His mind is especially active in the dark.

GAD. At least we won't have to look at that brightly
colored coat anymore. I'll splash blood on it and tear it
so it looks like an animal devoured him. We can take
it back to father and tell him this is all we found of
him. We don't know what happened. We just found
this in the wilderness. He must have been eaten by a
lion or bear.

DAN. *(looking L in the distance)* Hey, look what's
coming from the East. *(he points)*

ZEBULUN. What is it?

DAN. I don't know. They have several camels. I'll bet they're Ishmaelites on their trade route.

JUDAH. *(looking carefully)* Yes! Sure enough, here come the Ishmaelites. Let's sell Joseph to them! Why kill him and have a guilty conscience? We don't want to be responsible for his death. After all, he *is* our brother!

SIMEON. Let him die in the well, Judah. Why should we allow him to live, even as a slave?

ZEBULUN. Come on. Bring the boy out of the well and sell him to the Ishmaelites. We'll never see his face again, and we won't be responsible for his death. Let him live out his days as a slave. That'll teach him a lesson.

JUDAH. When the Ishmaelites come by, we can make them an offer. I say we sell him. What do you think?

BROTHERS. *(general assent and nodding of heads, with ad libs)* Sell the boaster. Who does he think he is? Let's get rid of him.

JUDAH. Here they come. Let me do the talking.

(Everybody waits a moment, looking toward L; JUDAH shouts to the ISHMAELITES.)

Hello, friends. Come this way! We want to talk to you.

(ISMAELITES enter from stage left, including five men.)

CHIEF ISHMAELITE. Hello. How are you doing? Are you from around here?

JUDAH. We are descendants of Abraham. We live in the land of Canaan. Our father is Jacob, and we are grazing our flocks here. We captured a thief and threw him into the well. We could let him die there, but if you're interested, we will sell him to you for twenty pieces of silver.

CHIEF ISHMAELITE. A thief? Show us the man.

JUDAH. Gad and Asher, go bring him up from the well.

(GAD and ASHER hurry off to get JOSEPH.)

CHIEF ISHMAELITE. How long have you been grazing here at Dothan?

JUDAH. For three days. We grazed at Shechem as well. There is plenty of grass on these slopes to fatten the bellies of our sheep! Where are you going with your cargo?

CHIEF ISHMAELITE. We're taking herbs and spices from Gilead to Egypt. There's a good market for our goods there.

(GAD and ASHER arrive, pulling JOSEPH at the end of a rope. JOSEPH is dirty. He is tied around his chest, waist, and arms with rope.)

JUDAH. Here's the hoodlum. He's strong and handsome, and should fetch a good price. He was caught stealing sheep.

CHIEF ISHMAELITE. *(walking around JOSEPH, sizing him up; he lifts his eyelids and checks his teeth)* He looks healthy enough. Yes, we will pay your price. Arpad, pay the man twenty pieces of silver. Thank you, friends. We'll get a good price for this one in Egypt. Now we must be on our way. God be with you.

JUDAH. Good-bye. And go with God.

ACT I, SCENE V

SCENE: *JACOB'S home. The brothers return to their father JACOB, carrying with them Joseph's torn and blood-spattered coat-of-many-colors. JACOB is sitting at his desk writing again, surrounded by his many wives, all busy with household duties. They are all knitting and sewing. The brothers enter with downcast expressions, and the eldest brother REUBEN acts as their spokesman to bring the bad news.*

REUBEN. *(speaking slowly with a heavy heart; REUBEN was not present when JOSEPH was sold to the ISHMAELITES, and he did not take part in the deal)* Father, we have some horrible news. We found this coat in the wilderness, torn and blood-stained, and we fear that it's Joseph's, since we heard that you sent him to find us in Shechem. Does it look like Joseph's coat? *(He hands JACOB the coat.)*

JACOB. *(examining the bloody coat carefully, his eyes frightened and filled with disbelief)* Yes, it *is* his coat! A wild animal must have attacked him. O God, no! My son Joseph! He's been torn in pieces! O God, have mercy! I'll die for the loss of my son. Joseph, my son! It can't be true. *(He falls to his knees, drops his face to the ground, and weeps. LEAH runs to comfort him, also crying. The other women stare in sorrow.)*

ACT I, SCENE VI

SCENE: *In POTIPHAR'S house where POTIPHAR is giving business instructions to JOSEPH. An elegant and beautifully dressed woman, POTIPHAR'S WIFE, is sitting at stage right combing her hair and making her face while she listens to the men talk. She is attended by a servant-girl who assists in beautifying her mistress. The men are at center stage, sitting on wooden chairs around a wooden table where they have some maps and papers spread out. POTIPHAR and JOSEPH are dressed in Egyptian clothing typical of the time, including skirts, loose open-necked shirts, and sandals.*

POTIPHAR. Do you think we should rotate the sheep to the North slopes next month, Joseph? They have been on the East side for three weeks.

JOSEPH. Yes. We don't want to graze the grass too low because the recovery rate is very slow when over-grazed.

POTIPHAR. You have a special touch in these matters. Our sheep have never grown so fat or reproduced in such large numbers under anyone else's care. You have brought me great prosperity! I will have to do something special at Christmas for those Ishmaelites who sold you to me.

JOSEPH. God has been faithful to answer my prayers.

POTIPHAR. And never have I seen a man seek God with such devotion. Your God has been pleased with you, I can tell. He rewards you well, and I will do the same.

JOSEPH. He has brought me through many trials, and has sustained my life despite many afflictions and misfortunes.

POTIPHAR. Tell me, how did a man who seems to have such favor with God become a lowly slave?

JOSEPH. My brothers despised me and sold me as a slave to an Ishmaelite caravan as it passed through Dothan.

POTIPHAR. Well, they must have been extremely angry to sell their own flesh and blood. What were they so mad about?

JOSEPH. My father gave me a coat-of-many-colors. It was a beautiful and expensive coat, and they thought I was father's favorite, so they despised me. They were jealous, I suppose. Then I told them about some dreams I had in which their sheaves bowed down to mine in the fields, and they were furious. They thought that I considered myself superior to them. I should have kept my dreams to myself.

POTIPHAR. For my sake I'm glad that they sold you. Their loss is my gain. But I'm sorry for you that you have suffered at the hands of your own family.

JOSEPH. God has sustained me through my trials. He has become both father and family to me, and you, sir, have likewise treated me with kindness and respect. I thank you for that.

POTIPHAR. Only a fool would do otherwise. I have benefited from the service you've given me. You have earned my admiration. You are obviously blessed of God, and because you work for me, I have benefited from your blessings.

JOSEPH. May the Lord continue to bless you and your house.

POTIPHAR. With you in control, I have no doubt that He will.

JOSEPH. I'll continue to seek His guidance.

POTIPHAR'S WIFE. Joseph has brought more grain to the fields and health to the flocks. My closets aren't large enough to hold my new clothes, and I haven't enough chests to hold my jewelry. Thank you, Joseph, for the prosperity you've brought to our house, and for the favor you've brought to my husband. Even Pharaoh has noticed that the captain of his guard is growing prosperous! Be careful--don't earn us so much wealth that you rouse the Pharaoh's envy.

JOSEPH. Give your thanks to the God of my fathers.

POTIPHAR'S WIFE. He must be a mighty God to know how to make a slave do so well! You might have been worked to death, but instead you have become assistant to Pharaoh's Chief Executioner! Because of you, my husband doesn't have a worry in the world.

POTIPHAR. Speaking of worries, I just might have one if I don't get myself moving. I'm nearly late for an appointment.

POTIPHAR'S WIFE. *(moving to her husband and giving him a warm embrace)* Be careful. I have ordered a fine feast for us tonight, so don't stay too late.

POTIPHAR. Good-bye, my sweet. *(He kisses her cheek.)*

(POTIPHAR exits UL.)

POTIPHAR'S WIFE. Joseph, let me fetch some cold grape juice and bring you something to eat.

(She exits UL; JOSEPH sits at table and works on papers; POTIPHAR'S wife enters UL carrying a large tray with fruit and two large mugs of wine. She takes the two large cups of wine in hand and then sits on long couch at center stage.)

Joseph, come talk with me. You can't spend all your time working. Come here and have some wine and fruit. I want to drink a toast to you, a toast of gratitude for the wonderful things you have brought to my home.

JOSEPH. *(walking to her, taking a cup from her hand; standing)* To Potiphar and his wife!

(They raise their mugs high and drink together.)

POTIPHAR'S WIFE. *(reclining on a couch in her long, beautiful gown)* Has some Hebrew woman in your homeland laid claim to your heart, Joseph?

JOSEPH. *(returning to his work at the table)* I have had no time for women. Slaves do not make good husbands, I'm afraid.

POTIPHAR'S WIFE. But you are no ordinary slave, Joseph. Surely you have some beautiful girl wooing your heart back home.

JOSEPH. My heart longs for my father and my family, but there is no woman drawing me homeward.

POTIPHAR'S WIFE. It seems such a pity to allow such strength to go unappreciated. What a waste! You should be the admiration of somebody!

JOSEPH. I have an entire flock of sheep who are devotedly attached to me.

POTIPHAR'S WIFE. Joseph, come here and sit with me. Put away those papers. You need to relax; it's good for your health. Here, have a fig. *(She walks sensuously to the table, collects some tidbits, strolls by JOSEPH where he's sitting, leans close to him, then takes him gently by the hand and returns to sit at center of couch. He follows, but sits at the far end of the couch as distant from her as possible. She looks disappointed, pauses, and goes to get the tray of fruit. She returns with it, and sits close to him.)* Try the honey-melon, Joseph. It's the sweetest. Here, let me pick one for you. I know the choicest pieces. *(She leans against him and takes her time picking through the plate of fruit until, after several moments, she finds one.)* Here, open that mouth of yours! Come on, open up!

(JOSEPH leans away from her and opens his mouth. She leans closer and pops in a piece of melon.)

JOSEPH. *(rising to his feet)* It's a sweet one! *(He returns to the desk and picks up papers.)*
POTIPHAR'S WIFE. *(She follows him quickly and takes the papers from his hand. She sets them on the table and holds up a handful of fruit.)* Have another piece, Joseph, and another, and another! *(She pops three in a row into his mouth. She giggles and moves closer to him, taking his hands in hers, looking into his eyes.)* O Joseph, hold me, hold me close. Joseph, please! *(She snuggles close to him.)*
JOSEPH. No, we can't do this! *(He casts her hands down gently but firmly, and crosses DL, determined to get away from her.)*
POTIPHAR'S WIFE. *(pursuing him)* But Joseph, I like you. I *want* you. Put your arms around me. *(She tugs him by the arms toward the couch.)* Come here, Joseph. I like you. Lay with me. Love me!
JOSEPH. *(pulling himself away, shaking his head violently)* No, I can't. And *you* can't. Have you lost your mind? Think of your husband! My master trusts me with everything in his house. He has given me authority over all his affairs! He has held back nothing from me except you, because you are his wife. How can I do a thing like this?
POTIPHAR'S WIFE. *(pulling at his clothes and arms)* Joseph, make love to me! Nobody will know.
(She caresses him.)
JOSEPH. *(pulling himself UL toward the door, trying to escape against her grasping and tugging at his outer shirt, which comes off in her hands as he moves toward the door)* No, let go of me! I can't do this. I have to go! *(He tears himself from her grasp and exits UL, leaving her holding his outer shirt.)*
POTIPHAR'S WIFE. *(She runs to the couch and collapses in tears, crying his name on the pillow. She stays there crying for awhile, then rises in frustration,*

pacing, thinking and plotting, and gradually grows angry. She lifts JOSEPH'S shirt to her face, then wads it into a ball. She makes an evil-eyed look as she gets an idea. She shakes out his shirt, stands, throws a few pillows on the floor, overturns the table, messes up her hair, tears some fabric at her neck, then screams, falls onto the couch, and begins shouting desperately.) Help! Help! Somebody help me! Help me! Rape! Joseph tried to rape me! Rape! Help!

(Several men and women hurry into the room, rushing to her assistance. They help her up.)

MAN-SERVANT. What happened?

(The ladies comfort her.)

POTIPHAR'S WIFE. That Hebrew slave Joseph tried to rape me! When I screamed he ran away. He left me holding his shirt! *(She holds up JOSEPH'S shirt.)*

MAN-SERVANT. Joseph tried to rape you? We'll find him!

(MANSERVANTS race out in pursuit of JOSEPH. FEMALE SERVANTS show sympathy and give support to POTIPHAR'S WIFE, seating her gently on the couch, gathering pillows to place behind her, examining her torn clothes, attending to her comfort.)

POTIPHAR'S WIFE. *(hysterically)* My husband had to bring in that Hebrew slave here to insult us! Go now, all of you. Leave me in peace. Let me rest. Send my husband to me immediately when he returns. Go now, all of you.

(FEMALE SERVANTS exit.)

ACT I, SCENE VII

SCENE: *POTIPHAR enters and hurries to his wife where she is reclining on the couch, pouting. He sits beside her. She rises on one elbow and gives him an embrace.*

POTIPHAR'S WIFE. *(standing, growing agitated, and speaking passionately)* Potiphar, Joseph tried to rape me! After you left he remained in the house and forced himself upon me. I screamed for help, so he ran off, leaving his shirt behind. Here it is. It was horrible! Hold me, my love!

(POTIPHAR holds his wife affectionately.)

POTIPHAR. *(astounded and angry, rising to his feet)* That traitor! I trusted him with all that I own! That ungrateful fool. He'll pay for this! After all I've done for him! So this is how he repays the man who trusts him to manage his house! *(He stomps his foot, and shouts for soldiers.)* Guards!

SOLDIERS. *(rushing in fully armed with swords)* Yes, my lord!

POTIPHAR. *(angrily)* Bring Joseph to me! He tried to rape my wife. He must pay heavily for this.

SOLDIERS. Yes, my lord.

(Soldiers rush out UL.)

POTIPHAR. *(Turning compassionately to his WIFE, looking into her eyes.)* I'm sorry, my love. I never dreamed he'd assault you. I'll put him far away in a dungeon so you will never see his face again.

POTIPHAR'S WIFE. *(curiously, quietly)* Where will you put him?

(Enter several soldiers, bringing Joseph bound before Potiphar.)

SOLDIERS. Here he is, my lord!

POTIPHAR. *(going to JOSEPH)* So you thought you could help yourself to my wife, did you! After I trusted you with all that I own. How could you do this, Joseph?

(JOSEPH starts to answer, but POTIPHAR lifts his hand to stop him.)

No! Don't speak to me. My wife told me everything.

POTIPHAR'S WIFE. *(sneeringly, while staring resentfully at JOSEPH)* You tried to rape me in my own home!

POTIPHAR. I never would have expected such a thing from someone as smart as you, but a man is not always what he seems. I would not have believed it if I had not heard it from my own wife. I am sorry to lose you, Joseph. You have served me well, but now you will serve in the palace prison for the rest of your days. My wife will never look upon you again. *(POTIPHAR'S WIFE is startled, gasps, but quickly turns it to approval.)* Good-bye, Joseph. I'm sorry that things had to end this way. What a sorry state of affairs. *(JOSEPH tries to speak, but POTIPHAR motions him to stop.)* Silence! Don't speak to me. I shall never hear your voice again. *(To the guards, loudly.)* Take him away!

(Guards exit with JOSEPH.)

ACT I, SCENE VIII

SCENE: *A prison. It's dark and cold. Furnishings include a wooden "bed" with no padding, a small table, and some hard stools or benches to sit upon. The King's CHIEF BAKER and his WINE TASTER sit dejected and morose, staring at the floor, in deep thought. The door is at R.*

JOSEPH. *(entering from R)* Good morning, men. *(He waits for a reply briefly then sets some bread and water on the bench. He looks at the two men, who remain slumped in posture, staring at the floor, speechless.)* I brought your breakfast in. *(pause, while JOSEPH studies them)* Better eat it while it's hot. *(He waits for them to respond to his humor. There is no response.)* It's roast mutton and fig muffins. Doesn't the former Chief Baker want to try the freshly-baked muffins? Of course, they're nothing like you could have baked.

BAKER. *(looks up and gives a faint smile)* Muffins, you say? Let's have a look. Who is the new Chief Baker, anyway? *(He walks over, examines a hard, stale hunk of bread critically and takes a drink of water from a crude wooden bowl. He holds the scrawny chunk of bread up to study it then bangs it on the table noisily.)* This muffin looks like a brick. *(He looks disgustedly at JOSEPH, then looks at the WINE TASTER who is staring dejectedly at the floor. He picks up the other bowl of water, examines it, winks at JOSEPH, then struts over to the WINE TASTER.)* Say Tipsy, could I bother Pharaoh's former Wine Taster for an opinion on the quality of some wine? *(He holds the bowl over the WINE TASTER'S head, looking serious.)*

WINE TASTER. *(looking up)* You have wine? For breakfast?

JOSEPH. *(innocently)* Breakfast? Why no, it's supper. You two have been so depressed you've lost track of both time and place.

BAKER. *(incredulously shaking his head)* I wouldn't go *that* far! This *does* still look a lot like a miserable jail, in spite of your efforts to make it pleasant, Joseph. But we *do* appreciate you, old boy. Since the jailor put you in charge of this poison-pit, things have greatly improved for us. Everyone appreciates your good spirit and the changes you've made. Tell me Joseph, how do you do it? Why aren't you filled with hatred like the rest of us?

JOSEPH. *(humbly)* Why make life more miserable than it already is? God is my only hope, and I look to Him. He gives me strength and comfort. I just thought you two looked a little down-in-the-mouth today. What's wrong?

BAKER. *(He looks at the WINE TASTER, who meets his gaze with a serious expression.)* We both had dreams last night, but there is no one to tell us what they mean.

JOSEPH. Interpreting dreams is God's business. Tell me what you saw.

WINE TASTER. These are not ordinary dreams, and it is very strange that we would both have similar dreams on the same night. Anyway, I hardly ever remember my dreams. It's weird.

BAKER. It must be some kind of sign from the gods. We don't know what to make of it.

WINE TASTER. And I don't like it one bit. But maybe you can make sense of it. Now listen carefully. in my dream I saw a vine with three branches that began to bud and blossom, and soon there were clusters of ripe grapes. I was holding Pharaoh's wine cup in my hand, so I took the grapes and squeezed the juice into it, and gave it to him to drink.

JOSEPH. *(pausing, pondering briefly)* I know what the dream means. The three branches mean three days! Within three days Pharaoh is going to take you out of prison and give you back your job as his wine taster. Please have some pity on me when you are back in his favor, and mention me to Pharaoh, and ask him to let me out of here. For I was kidnapped from my homeland among the Hebrews, and now I am in jail when I did nothing to deserve it.

BAKER. *(standing, looking hopeful)* Ha, that's not a bad dream at all! Tell me what mine means, Joseph. In my dream there were three baskets of pastries on my head. In the top basket were all kinds of bakery goods for Pharaoh, but the birds came and ate them.

JOSEPH. *(Thoughtfully pausing, and looking grim; speaking carefully and sadly)* I'm sorry to say this, but this is what it means. The three baskets mean three days. Three days from now Pharaoh will take off your head and impale your body on a pole, and the birds will come and pick off your flesh!

BAKER. *(looking appalled and sick, and speaking up to the heavens)* O you gods, have mercy on my soul! *(He looks intently at JOSEPH, studying his face and looking askance at him, as if he hopes to hear some alteration of the interpretation, or some better news added.)* But how can you know such a thing? This is nothing but reckless speculation. You're wrong, Joseph. There's no way to know such things. You're guessing.

JOSEPH. *(sadly but firmly)* God has shown me the interpretation, and it will happen as I said. I'm sorry to be the one to tell you.

BAKER.   You're only a slave.   What do you know?
     Nothing! *(His voice rises slowly until he shouts.)* The
     dreams will come to nothing, I tell you!   You're
     wrong! Keep your foolish ideas to yourself.
JOSEPH.   The fear of the LORD is the beginning of
     wisdom! If I were you, I would plead for mercy, my
     friend. *(placing his hand on the Baker's shoulder)*
BAKER.   To whose Lord, Joseph? Yours?   There are
     many gods. Why should one god be feared more than
     another?
JOSEPH. There is but one true God, and all things belong
     to Him. May He have mercy on us all!
BAKER.   *(looking to heaven with a face of terror, and
     begging frantically)* O great god of the sun, have
     mercy on me! Mighty Ra, do not let me die! *(He falls
     to his knees, begging for mercy, then collapses on his
     face.)*
(Lights fade.)

ACT I, SCENE IX

SCENE: *A room in the palace of PHARAOH, King of Egypt.   PHARAOH is having a birthday party attended by his officials and his household staff, consisting of six to ten sundry characters.   They are dressed for frivolity in colorful costumes. The ladies have long flowing gowns in Egyptian style, and the men are dressed handsomely. Three musicians are playing cheerful pieces on lutes, flutes, and coronets. There is food and lively conversation briefly as the scene opens.   The men are laughing with their women. Fresh fruit, figs, grapes, melons, meats, and wine is plentiful, as is being passed out by female servants who are dressed in simple white gowns.*

PHARAOH. Attention!
(Everybody looks to PHARAOH, and the music and conversation stop.)
Today is a happy day! We celebrate the abundance of our
   crops and the good fortune which the sun god Ra has
   bestowed upon us. Let us drink a toast to our great
   god Ra! *(lifting his glass, with everybody doing
   likewise, and shouting with the King)* To the sun god
   Ra!
(Everybody drinks.)
And now I have some business at hand. The Captain of the
   Guard has brought the Wine Taster and the Chief
   Baker from prison, and they stand here before you.
   Let this day be an example for those who serve
   Pharaoh of Egypt, that none shall betray their King, or
   the duty to which they have been called. *(PHARAOH*

points at the two men standing UL, guarded by POTIPHAR, dressed as a soldier, and armed with an imposing sword.) These men were imprisoned under suspicion of espionage, and their cases have been studied carefully by my lawyers. Today I wish to restore my faithful Wine Taster to his position in the palace.

(There is general applause.)

WINE TASTER. *(Breaking into a broad smile, and speaking with immense relief and gratitude.)* O thank you, mighty Pharaoh! *(WINE TASTER falls to one knee, lifts his hands to the heavens, and shouts.)* May the Pharaoh live forever! *(responding all together, the entire crowd lifts their right arms high and shouts in unison)* May the Pharaoh live forever!

PHARAOH. The Chief Baker, however, has been found guilty of conspiracy against his King. His head shall be taken off at dawn and his body impaled upon a pole until the birds have picked the flesh from his bones! Pharaoh has spoken. Let it be done. And let all take heed, and remain forever faithful.

BAKER. *(falling to his knees, pleading for his life in a desperate tone of voice)* O Mighty Pharaoh, have mercy! Spare my life. I am innocent! I will serve you forever.

POTIPHAR. Stand to your feet and hold your tongue! *(He lifts him roughly to his feet and raises the sword to his throat.)* Away with you! *(He pushes him toward the doorway R, accompanied by two armed guards.)*

ACT I, SCENE X

SCENE: *The palace of PHAROAH.   The King is surrounded by two wise men, two magicians, a servant, and his WINE TASTER whom he has called to give him counsel concerning some matters deeply troubling him. He is sitting on his throne, and the counselors are standing, prepared to give counsel.   Two years have passed since the last scene. The door is R.*

PHARAOH. I have had a dream and I need somebody to interpret it for me. I am deeply troubled by what I have seen.

FIRST WISE MAN.   Interpreting dreams is tricky business. How can anyone know for certain what it means. How can it be proven? I would not venture to interpret Pharaoh's dream.

FIRST MAGICIAN. The logical mind cannot discern the meaning of dreams, for dreams are spiritual in nature. Tell us your dream, and we will try to interpret it spiritually.   *(He gestures toward the SECOND MAGICIAN as if they are a team.)*

PHARAOH. I was standing on the bank of the Nile River when suddenly seven fat, healthy-looking cows came up out of the river and began grazing along the river bank. But then seven other cows came up from the river, very skinny and bony. And these skinny cattle ate up the seven fat ones that had come out first, and afterwards they were still as skinny as before! Then I woke up. That is the first part. *(He looks at the magicians, expecting a reply.)*

FIRST MAGICIAN. *(glancing at the SECOND MAGICIAN, then consulting in a whisper briefly with him)* It is a peculiar dream, and we cannot say what it means.

SECOND MAGICIAN. It is not a dream whose symbols are in keeping with standard dream analysis.

WINE TASTER. *(suddenly aroused and blurting out an announcement, speaking to PHARAOH)* Wait! I just remembered something important. Two years ago when you were angry and put me and the Chief Baker in jail, the Second Magician and I each had a dream one night. We told the dreams to a Hebrew fellow there who had been a slave of the Captain of the Guard. He told us what our dreams meant. He interpreted them, and everything happened just as he said. I was restored to my position as Wine Taster, and the Chief Baker was executed and impaled on a pole, poor fellow.

PHARAOH. Who was this Hebrew slave?

WINE TASTER. His name was Joseph. He was so well liked by the jailer that Joseph was placed in command of everything. The jailor had an easy time of it.

PHARAOH. *(turning to his servant)* Send to the palace prison and have this man brought to me immediately.

SERVANT. *(bowing)* I will, Mighty One.

(The servant exits R.)

PHARAOH. *(rubbing his cheeks and chin, pondering his problems)* Maybe this man can tell me the meaning of my dream. I can't rest at all until I have an interpretation.

FIRST MAGICIAN. I doubt very much that some Hebrew slave brought to you from prison will be able to interpret Pharaoh's dream!

SECOND MAGICIAN. *(mockingly)* How can we believe what is said by a slave coming out of prison? How could such a fellow be trusted?

FIRST WISE MAN. *(nodding)* He has been imprisoned for breaking the law. Is it likely that he will be honest, or educated, or intelligent?

SECOND WISE MAN. *(smiling with a look of tolerant indulgence)* He would be a fool not to venture some kind of guess, no matter how far fetched. He has little to lose by guessing, and little to gain by rejecting the invitation.

PHARAOH. *(with a stern expression of correction)* I did not send an invitation! I sent a *command.* Do not be so quick to judge other men. Many a wise man has found himself locked in prison, which is precisely what may befall all of you advisors if I don't get something more than empty blabber and weak excuses!

FIRST WISE MAN. *(bowing)* Yes, Mighty One.

FIRST MAGICIAN. Are you aware that the Hebrew people worship a god that has no name? And only *one* god at that!

SECOND WISE MAN. *(smiling)* It is a poor people who have but one god.

(Servant enters R with JOSEPH.)

SERVANT. *(bowing to PHARAOH)* Here is the man, Mighty Pharaoh.

PHARAOH. *(examining JOSEPH closely)* You are Joseph, the Hebrew slave?

(JOSEPH bows and nods.)

I have been told that you are able to interpret dreams. Is this true?

JOSEPH. *(speaking boldly)* I can't do it myself, but God can reveal secret and hidden things.

PHARAOH. *(pausing, looking carefully JOSEPH at and the others)* None of these men can tell me what my dream means. That is why I have called for you.

JOSEPH. *(standing tall)* Tell me your dream, and perhaps God will reveal the meaning to me.

PHARAOH. I was standing upon the bank of the Nile River when suddenly seven fat, healthy-looking cows came up out of the river and began grazing along the river bank. But then several other cows came up from the river, very skinny and bony--in fact, I've never seen such poor-looking specimens in all the land of Egypt. These skinny cattle ate up the seven fat ones that had come out first, and afterwards they were still as skinny as before! Then I woke up. Later I had another dream. This time there were seven heads of grain on one stalk, and all seven heads were plump and full. Then, out of the same stalk, came seven withered, thin heads. And the thin heads swallowed up the fat ones! Now, can you tell me the meaning of this?

JOSEPH. Both dreams mean the same thing. God was telling you what He is going to do here in the land of Egypt. The seven fat cows and the seven well-formed heads of grain mean that there are seven years of prosperity ahead. The seven skinny cows and also the seven withered heads of grain indicate that there will be seven years of famine following the seven years of prosperity. So God has shown you what he is about to do. The next seven years will be a period of great prosperity throughout all the land of Egypt, but afterwards there will be seven years of famine so great that all the prosperity will be wiped out. Famine will consume the land. My suggestion is that you find the wisest man in Egypt and put him in charge of administering a nation-wide farm program. Let Pharaoh divide Egypt into five administrative districts, and let the officials of these districts gather into the royal storehouses all the excess crops of the next seven years, so that there will be enough to eat when the seven years of famine come. Otherwise, disaster will surely strike.

PHARAOH. *(staring intently at Joseph, pondering what has been said, looking around at the others)* These are powerful words you speak, Joseph. How do you know you are right?

JOSEPH. I do not interpret your dream myself, but the God of my people has revealed the meaning for the benefit of Pharaoh and all of Egypt.

PHARAOH. You answer well for a man brought out of prison. What crime have you committed?

JOSEPH. I committed no crime. I was purchased as a slave by Ishmaelites and sold to Potiphar, Captain of the Guard.

PHARAOH. *(coming to an awareness)* O yes, Potiphar's wife. I've heard the story. *(turning to his magicians and wise men)* What do you make of what the man has said?

FIRST WISE MAN. How can it be confirmed or refuted? There is no way to know.

SECOND WISE MAN. It has some sense to it. It would be difficult to invent such an idea so quickly.

FIRST MAGICIAN. This man would make a fine statesman for Pharaoh. He thinks quickly on his feet, and is an able speaker. But we would be a fool to trust him. I suggest we appoint a committee to consider it more fully and to judge the merits of the case.

SECOND MAGICIAN. There is something intuitive in me which wants to believe the man. It seems right that the concept of the seven fat cows should be reinforced with the seven fat heads of grain. It is not customary for a mad man to repeat himself in such rational renditions of reinforcing symbols.

SECOND WISE MAN. He has spoken well, and nobody else has been able to come up with any interpretation. Perhaps the Hebrew is correct and the sun god Ra is telling Pharaoh what will come to pass so that Pharaoh can save his people. It makes sense. Pharaoh would be greatly esteemed for making preparations in advance of a great famine!

FIRST WISE MAN. That is true. We have nothing better to suppose. The Wine Taster testified that what Joseph said about he and the Chief Baker came to pass. Perhaps he has a gift from the gods to interpret dreams, and the man has been placed in Pharaoh's prison for this very occasion.

PHARAOH. *(turning to JOSEPH)* I too am persuaded by you, Joseph. You say that I should find someone to put in charge of administering a farm program. *(sizing up Joseph, and looking around at each of his counselors)* Who could do it better than Joseph? He is a man who is obviously filled with the Spirit of God. *(turning to JOSEPH and speaking directly to him)* Since God has revealed the meaning of my dreams to you, you are the wisest man in the country! I hereby appoint you to be in charge of this entire project. What you say goes, throughout all the land of Egypt. I alone will outrank you. *(He takes a ring off his finger and places it on JOSEPH'S hand.)* Take this signet ring as a token of my authority. *(He picks up a royal cape of purple resting on the seat of the throne, and places it on JOSEPH'S shoulders. Then he takes the royal golden chain from about his neck and places it on JOSEPH.)* Behold, I have placed you in charge of all the land of Egypt!

ACT II, SCENE I

SCENE: *JACOB'S home in the land of Canaan. The entire land is suffering severely from the famine, and JACOB and his sons have been considering what to do about the situation. The men are sitting and standing in Jacob's home, some on couches, some on benches, stools, and chairs. They have no food to eat, but they are drinking large amounts of water to make up for the loss of more substantial things to fill their bellies.*

JACOB. We cannot spend our days endlessly discussing our desperate and hopeless situation. Why are you standing around looking at one another? I have heard that there is grain in Egypt. We can't live on water alone. Go down and buy grain for us before we all starve to death.

REUBEN. Yes, father, I suppose we must. But it's a long journey and there is no telling what might happen.

JACOB. *(nodding his head)* True, my son, but we shall all perish debating the matter endlessly and complaining about our circumstances. Take your brothers and go to Egypt and bring us food. We cannot sit here idle and watch our women and children die before our eyes. But leave little Benjamin here with me. You cannot take him, for if something were to happen to him, I would surely die of sorrow. My son Joseph is dead already, and if the other son of my old age were to be taken from me I wouldn't be able to bear it. You ten brothers pack the camels and prepare for the journey, leaving as soon as you can. God go

with you. Be careful, and return in haste to your families. We will all wait anxiously for your return. May the LORD OF HOSTS have mercy on us! Now go, all of you, and leave me in peace. I do not want you to go, but I cannot allow us all to starve here while we do nothing. Go--let me rest now! *(He waves them off with a loving display of frustrated affection; all exit.)*
(Lights fade.)

ACT II, SCENE II

SCENE: *A street near JOSEPH'S quarters in Egypt where grain is stored.   JOSEPH'S ten older brothers have just arrived. They are dressed in long robes and headgear to protect them from the desert wind and sun. They are weary and weak as they arrive to purchase grain. They stop in the streets to ask where they should go to buy the grain.*

REUBEN. *(entering UR and walking up to a group of local people talking on the street at C)* Excuse me, but could you help us, please? We have come from the land of Canaan to buy grain. Can you tell us where to find the storehouse?

EGYPTIAN. *(turning from his friends to talk)* So the famine has touched the land of Canaan too, has it? People from everywhere are coming to Egypt to buy food.

REUBEN. Our father sent us here before the family starves to death. We must return quickly to save the ones we left behind. You are lucky to live in a land that's prepared for this devastation.

EGYPTIAN. Pharaoh has stored mountains of grain! He was told by a wise man who interpreted a dream which was given to Pharaoh by the gods. We are greatly favored among the nations.

REUBEN. Which way do we go?

EGYPTIAN. Continue on this road into the heart of the city. The granaries are behind the temple of the sun god Ra, beyond the palace of Pharaoh. You will see a great wall. Follow it to the gates and someone will show you what to do.

REUBEN. Thank you.

EGYPTIAN. I hope you make it home in time to save your family. Good luck to you. *(He waves them off.)*

ACT II, SCENE III

SCENE: *Administrative room at the storehouse of grain where JOSEPH and two advisers are standing center stage, surrounded by four soldiers, fully armed, and two female servants who are ready with cups of water and large fans with which they waft the air. A clerk is sitting at a table DL, recording transactions on a large scroll of papyrus. REUBEN and his brothers are met at the door UL and led before JOSEPH.*

REUBEN. *(bowing together with his brothers so that they are on their knees with their foreheads touching the ground before them, fulfilling the prophecy revealed to JOSEPH in his childhood dream)* Greetings, Great One. We have come to request that you sell us grain to save the lives of our family.

JOSEPH. *(He recognizes his brothers instantly, but pretends that he doesn't. He studies them carefully for a few moments, then motions to one of the female servants to bring him a drink, permitting him time to think before speaking. Finally he speaks gruffly.)* Where are you men from?

REUBEN. *(cautiously speaking)* From the land of Canaan, my lord.

JOSEPH. *(suddenly remembering the dreams of long ago and exploding with an accusation)* So, you are spies! You have come to see how destitute the famine has made us.

REUBEN. *(stepping back in fear and amazement)* No, my lord! We have come to buy food. We are all brothers and honest men. We are not spies!

(The other brothers nod their heads in agreement.)

JOSEPH. *(angrily)* You are spies! You have come to see how weak our nation has become.

REUBEN. *(appealing politely)* No, not at all! Sir, please hear me--there are twelve of us brothers, and our father is in the land of Canaan. Our youngest brother is there with our father, and one of our brothers is dead.

JOSEPH. Is that so? What does that prove? *(pausing, thinking)* How do I know if what you say is true? This is how I will test your story. I swear by the life of Pharaoh that you will not leave Egypt until your youngest brother comes here. One of you must go and get your brother! I'll keep the rest of you here in prison until Benjamin arrives. Then we'll find out whether your story is true. If it turns out that you don't have a younger brother, then I'll know that you are spies. *(turning to the soldiers, he commands them in a harsh tone)* Lock the men in the palace prison!

(Six soldiers draw their weapons and push the brothers out the door UL.)

ACT II, SCENE IV

SCENE: *Same as last scene. JOSEPH is center stage, surrounded by his advisers, soldiers, and servants. The clerk works at his desk, writing, calculating, and tallying the books. As JOSEPH discusses business with an adviser, several additional soldiers enter with the brothers, bringing them before JOSEPH.*

JOSEPH. *(looking at them sternly, standing tall)* I'm a God-fearing man and I've decided to give you an opportunity to prove yourselves. I'm going to take a chance that you are honorable. Only one of you shall remain here in jail, and the rest of you may go on home with grain to your families. But you must bring your youngest brother back to me! In this way I will know whether you are telling me the truth. If you are, I will spare you.

MESSENGER. *(running in at door UL)* My lord, a message from Pharaoh!

JOSEPH. *(extending his arm toward the messenger)* Bring it to me.

(Messenger does so and then exits UL.)

(JOSEPH reads the message, then turns aside from the brothers and motions his advisers to consult with him UR. The brothers, upon seeing JOSEPH occupied, move DL and speak audibly to one another without allowing to JOSEPH hear them, but JOSEPH notices them.)

REUBEN. *(motioning his brothers closer to him)* This has all happened because of what we did to Joseph. We saw his terror and heard his pleading, but we wouldn't listen! Didn't I tell you not to do it? But you wouldn't listen. Now we are going to die because we murdered him!

(JOSEPH, noticing the brothers talking together, turns an ear toward them in time to hear REUBEN'S remarks. He is so moved by what he hears that he moves DC grasping his throat as he is choked up. In a few moments he recovers.)

JOSEPH. *(speaking to the soldiers)* Bind that man and take him to the prison! *(He points to SIMEON, who is bound before their eyes and taken away UL.)* Order the servants at the granary to fill the sacks of the other men with grain, and give them provisions for their journey home. Now go, all of you, except my captain. *(He motions to his captain to come close as everybody exits. He waits until they are alone; to his captain.)* Put each of the men's payments at the top of his sack after they are filled with grain.

(The captain bows and exits quickly. JOSEPH walks to the clerk's table DL, stares at the papers a moment, then sweeps them off the table in frustration.)

ACT II, SCENE V

SCENE: *In the wilderness on their journey home, the brothers are resting at camp. They recline on the ground on their blankets, talking, eating, and drinking.*

JUDAH.   *(rushing in from R with a pouch of money; shouting with alarm)* Look! I opened my sack to get grain for my donkey and I found my money at the top of the sack! It's all here! What is going on?
(All the brothers rush over to look at the bag of money, trembling with fear and confusion.)
GAD. *(frightened)* What is God doing to us?
LEVI.   Things that have been happening lately cannot possibly be by chance. We experience one strange event after another. We're in the hands of God.
(The brothers look nervously at one another.)

ACT II, SCENE VI

SCENE: *JACOB'S home in the land of Canaan. LEAH, ZILPAH, and BILHAH are busy with household chores as before. They are talking about the famine and the depleted food supply.*

BILHAH. *(looking up from her sewing; to LEAH)* I don't think we have enough food to last another week, Leah. What are we going to do? Jacob prays and prays and the famine grows greater every day. Are we just going to slowly starve to death?

LEAH. I don't know why the LORD doesn't answer our prayers. Is He punishing us for something? All the joy has gone from our lives. We have no food, no fun, and no festivities!

BILHAH. No new clothes, no shopping. I've never been so bored in my life! We never have any fun!

LEAH. Jacob is in such bad spirits. He never laughs anymore. All the men are preoccupied with their problems. I can't even interest Jacob in *being* with me anymore!

BILHAH. If he's not spending time with *you*, then who *is* he spending time with? *(She looks inquiringly at ZILPAH.)*

ZILPAH. Don't look at *me*! I await the command of my mistress before getting involved in such things!

BILHAH. That's for sure! Only on direct orders would I get near the man! *(smiling)* I wouldn't *object* if called for me, of course.

LEAH. I don't think he'll be calling for any of us in the near future, girls. But thanks for your *willingness*. I think Jacob is so depressed he can't even *think* about romance these days. He hasn't been with anyone since the day I *hired* him with my son's mandrakes.

ZILPAH. *(eagerly)* *I'll* trade you some mandrakes for a night with Jacob, Leah.

BILHAH. Show us the mandrakes first.

LEAH. *(mockingly)* I don't think we have the power to bargain him away these days, Zilpah. He isn't exactly whistling for any of us, is he?

BILHAH. *(arrogantly, lifting her chin and giving her hair a toss)* If anybody was able to attract that man's attention, it was Rachel!

LEAH. *(mockingly)* Rachel, Rachel, the fairest of five thousand, the apple of his eye!

(JACOB and BENJAMIN enter. JACOB sits at his desk center stage. BENJAMIN stands beside him, observing.)

JACOB. Good day, ladies.

(The women look wonderingly at him, continuing their chores in silence.)

BILHAH. Hello, my sweet.

(She walks to him and kisses his cheek.)

LEAH. Hello, my mighty man. *(She gives him a kiss too, then turns to ZILPAH.)* Don't *you* get any ideas!

JACOB. Are you all having a good day?

(They look disgustedly at one another, rolling their eyes. Suddenly a loud commotion is heard from outside. JACOB'S sons come boisterously into the room UR.)

REUBEN. *(rushing in first)* Father, we're home! We're home and we brought lots of food! Our donkeys are loaded with grain.

(All the brothers approach JACOB and BENJAMIN to exchange greetings.)

JACOB. *(with joy)* Welcome home, boys! Ha ha! So God has brought you safely home! The LORD be praised! How have you been? *(He grasps his sons one at a time, holding them by the arms and giving each a warm embrace.)* Wonderful! So good to see you! *(to LEAH)* Leah, let's have a celebration! Gather the servants and prepare a feast. Take grain from the donkeys and make cakes and pies and bread, whatever you wish. This is a happy day!

(LEAH exits UR.)

LEVI. *(clapping his hands in glee)* And bring the musicians! It's time to hear some good old Hebrew music!

ASHER. We have more stuff than grain on our donkeys, father.

GAD. There's fruit, figs, raisins, and pomegranates!

ISSACHAR. How nice it will be to discuss religion with somebody who knows our law! And I can study my books in peace and quiet for once.

ZEBULUN. I want to hear Hebrew songs and see our women dance!

JACOB. In good time. But first, Reuben, tell me about your travels, and how you obtained the food.

REUBEN. *(cringing slightly, looking at his brothers with uneasiness)* Our travels were safe and we bought the grain, father, but everything did not go as we had hoped. Some things happened that we don't understand. We can't figure it out. We were caught up in the strangest circumstances. To begin with, Simeon is not with us. He remains in Egypt.

JACOB. *(shocked)* Simeon is still in *Egypt*? Why?

REUBEN. *(sheepishly)* Father, I'm so sorry! He's being held in prison by Pharaoh's assistant.

JACOB. *(outraged; shouting angrily)* Simeon's in prison? Why? What has he done?

REUBEN. Pharaoh's chief assistant was suspicious of us for no reason at all. He spoke very roughly to us from the very beginning. He thought we were spies. "No, no," we told him, "We are honest men, not spies. We are twelve brothers, sons of one father. One is dead, and the youngest is with our father in the land of Canaan." Then the man said, "I will find out if you are what you say you are. Leave one of your brothers with me and take grain to your families, but bring your youngest brother back to me. Then I'll know whether you are spies or honest men. If you prove to be what you say, I'll give you back your brother and you can come as often as you like to purchase grain."

JACOB. *(pounding his fist on a table and shouting)* No! He wants Benjamin? He wants Benjamin to go to Egypt? What has happened to bring this upon us?

JUDAH. The man was extremely suspicious and unreasonable from the beginning, father. We pled desperately with him to let us come home or we would still be there in the prison. It was God's mercy that he only kept *one* of us!

JACOB. God's *mercy*! I don't understand. You must have lied or stolen something. Swear to me that you are telling the truth!

JUDAH. Father, we *are* telling the truth. The man took us for spies for no reason. We have discussed it a hundred times and can't understand it!

JACOB. It's incredible! It's not possible! Reuben, is it true what Judah has said?

REUBEN. Yes, father. Judah is telling the truth. I'm sorry to say it.

JACOB. It is a strange day that brings both good news and bad. My sons return with grain to save us from starvation, and tell me that Simeon is held in the prison of Pharaoh. *(looking to the heavens, falling to his knees)* O MIGHTY LORD! Remember the promises you gave to Abraham, to Isaac, and to me. Save my son Simeon from the hand of Pharaoh. Don't break my heart, O God!

LEAH.   *(running in, speaking frantically)*   Jacob, the servants have opened the sacks of grain. At the top of every sack we found the money we sent to pay for it!

JACOB. The money is in the sacks? How can that be? Reuben, what does this mean?

REUBEN. Father, I don't know! We too opened one of the sacks and found money there, but we didn't know about the others. We *paid* for the grain—of course we did! It doesn't make sense. It must be something that God has done!

JACOB. *(looking up desperately)* LORD, is it *you*? *(turning to REUBEN angrily)* Reuben, you have bereaved me of my children. Long ago Joseph never came back, and Simeon is gone, and now you want to take Benjamin! Everything has gone against me!

REUBEN. *(passionately)* Kill my two sons if I don't bring Benjamin back to you. I'll be responsible for him.

JACOB. *(with determination)* No! Benjamin shall *not* go down with you, for his brother Joseph is dead, and Benjamin alone is left of his mother Rachel's children. If something should happen to him, I would surely die!

ACT II, SCENE VII

SCENE: *Same as previous scene, but three months later. JACOB and his sons are gathered in the house, discussing their situation.*

JACOB. It has been three months since you returned from Egypt, and the grain you bought is nearly gone. We can't wait any longer. We must do something. Go again to Egypt and buy us more food.

JUDAH. The man wasn't fooling when he said, "Don't ever come back unless your brother is with you." We cannot go unless you let Benjamin go with us.

JACOB. *(with frustrated anger)* What is this? Why did you ever tell him you had another brother? Why did you have to treat me like that? *(He looks each son intently in the face.)*

JUDAH. But the man specifically asked us about our family. He wanted to know whether our father was still living, and he asked us if we had another brother, so we told him. How could we know that he was going to say, "Bring me your other brother?" Father, just send the boy with me and we will go to Egypt. Otherwise we will all die of starvation, and not only we, but you and all our little ones. I will guarantee his safety. If I don't bring him back to you, then let me bear the blame forever. We could have gone and returned by now if you had permitted it.

REUBEN. Father, listen to us. Judah is right. All of us will die if we don't return to Egypt, and the man will sell us nothing if we don't take Benjamin. We have no choice. We must do it or stay here and die.

ISSACHAR. We have considered the situation for months now, father, and we all know what has to be done. God will go with us, and we will return with food and with Simeon. The LORD will bring us back safely.

JACOB. *(considering seriously, pondering, then speaking slowly)* Ah, if it cannot be avoided, then at least do this. Load your donkeys with the best products of the land. Take them to the man as gifts--balm, honey, spices, myrrh, pistachio nuts, and almonds. Take double money so you can pay back what was in the mouths of your sacks, as it was probably someone's mistake. Take your brother Benjamin and go. May God Almighty give you mercy before the man, so that he will release Simeon and return Benjamin home safely. And if I must bear the anguish of their deaths, then so be it. I can do no other. *(He walks to a chair DL and sits dejectedly.)*

(The brothers go to him one at a time and put a hand on his shoulder in a reluctant attempt to say farewell. They exit one-by-one UR.)

(Lights go out.)

ACT II, SCENE VIII

SCENE: *JOSEPH'S quarters in Egypt. The sons have come to meet JOSEPH and to purchase more grain.*

JOSEPH. *(standing center stage, surrounded by his soldiers, servants, wise men, magicians, and clerk)* So you have come back from the land of Canaan and you have brought your younger brother with you! Then you are indeed honest men, and not spies. Bring the young one before me.

(REUBEN brings BENJAMIN before JOSEPH. He immediately recognizes him and is deeply moved, assuming a serious expression and speaking hurriedly so as to dismiss them. He turns to the FIRST WISE MAN and speaks.)

These men will eat with me this noon. Take them to my home and instruct my servants to prepare a great feast!

(FIRST WISE MAN exits UL.)

(The brothers show alarm, looking at one another in fear, not knowing the meaning of this event. JOSEPH motions his servants and assistants to come UL and hear instructions from him. Meanwhile the brothers move DR and talk in a fashion that JOSEPH cannot hear, but the audience can.)

ASHER. *(speaking quietly to the brothers gathered closely around him)* It's because of the money that was returned to us in our sacks. He wants to say we stole it so he can seize us as slaves.

GAD. We will be slaves in his house forever and father will never hear from us again. God is repaying us for the way we treated Joseph.

LEVI. It must be true. How else could everything go so badly? We have the worst luck in the world.

JUDAH. Father will die in sorrow if we don't return. I can't believe it! Nothing goes right!

JOSEPH. *(turning from his servants to speak to the brothers)* My servant will lead you to my house. Follow this man. I will be there at noon.

(One of the servants leads the brothers out of the room UL. JOSEPH looks to the heavens.)

O LORD my God, how mighty is your hand! You are a God of grace and mercy!

ACT II, SCENE IX

SCENE: *At JOSEPH'S home. Three tables are set for a feast. Two of the tables are large enough to seat eight, and the other is for two. Much fruit, bread, meat, and drink are set on the table. The scene is festive. MUSICIANS are playing UL at various times.*

REUBEN. *(led by JOSEPH'S HOUSE MANAGER into the room from UR to C with his brothers following; speaking to the HOUSE MANAGER)* Sir, after our first trip to Egypt to buy food, as we were returning home, we stopped for the night and opened our sacks, and the money was there that we had paid for the grain. Here it is. We have brought it back again, along with additional money to buy more grain. We have no idea how the money got into our sacks.

HOUSE MANAGER. Don't worry about it. Your God must have put it there, for we collected your money as we should.

(All the brothers hear this and look relieved. A servant enters UR with SIMEON following, and SIMEON runs to his brothers eagerly. They embrace excitedly and exchange greetings.)

Your brother Simeon is now free to join you. As you see he is in good health. He has been well cared for.

REUBEN. This is wonderful. We truly thank you!

(The brothers nod in agreement.)

(JOSEPH enters UR. All the brothers bow low before him.)

JOSEPH. I see your brother Simeon has joined you! You are all together at last. And how is your father, the old man you spoke about? Is he still alive?

JUDAH. Yes, he is alive and well.

JOSEPH. *(walking up to BENJAMIN and examining him closely)* And this is your youngest brother, the one you told me about? How are you, my son? God be gracious to you. *(JOSEPH pats him on the shoulders with both hands and gives a broad smile. He then runs from the room out door UR to prevent an emotional outburst. The brothers look at one another, shrugging their shoulders in bewilderment.)*

REUBEN. *(speaking to the HOUSE MANAGER)* Please excuse us to go out and get the gifts we have brought for your master.

HOUSE MANAGER. You may go, but don't be gone long. The meal is prepared.

REUBEN. They're just outside.

(The brothers exit UL and return with numerous sacks filled with food and gifts.)

JOSEPH. *(entering UR, looking composed and refreshed, wearing brightly colored clothing reminiscent to his coat-of-many-colors)* Now let's eat! The Hebrews will sit at that table *(pointing to the table center stage)*, the Egyptians will eat at that one *(pointing to the table at L)*, and I will eat at this one *(pointing to the small table R where he will eat alone)*. Servants, fill the men's plates with whatever they like, and don't be stingy. And give the youngest brother five times as much as the others!

(BENJAMIN and the brothers all look surprised, and shrug their shoulders once again at things they cannot comprehend. Joseph speaks to the musicians.)

Make music! *(MUSICIANS begin playing.)* There's more wine in the casks than anyone can drink, so fill your goblets full!

(Everybody reaches for fruit already placed at the center of each table, and the servants begin taking trays full of food to each person, heaping the food especially high upon BENJAMIN'S plate.   Music and conversation grow increasingly animated as the food and wine begin to flow freely.)

ACT II, SCENE X

SCENE: *JOSEPH is in his home with his HOUSE MANAGER.*

JOSEPH. *(speaking to his HOUSE MANAGER)* The Hebrew men are ready to return to their country. Here's what I want you to do. Fill each of their sacks with as much grain as they can carry. Then put into the mouth of each man's sack the money he paid for the grain. I am giving it to them. Put my own silver cup at the top of young Benjamin's sack, along with the grain money.

HOUSE MANAGER. Yes, my lord! You are most gracious to these men, I must say!

JOSEPH. There is a special purpose in all of this, and they will surely be surprised when they learn what it is!

HOUSE MANAGER. I know that they are baffled by your behavior. Indeed, all your dealings with them seem peculiar to all of us, my lord.

JOSEPH. You will learn the meaning of it in good time. Be patient, and you shall behold the glory of God!

HOUSE MANAGER. Your God favors you greatly. Serving you has proven good duty. I have seen strange and wonderful things, my lord.

(HOUSE MANAGER exits UL.)

ACT 2, SCENE XI

SCENE: *At JOSEPH'S house again a few days later. JOSEPH is speaking with his HOUSE MANAGER.*

JOSEPH. The Hebrews are one day's journey toward the land of Canaan. Chase after them and stop them. Ask them why they are acting like this when their benefactor has been so kind to them. Ask them, "What do you mean by stealing my lord's silver drinking cup which he uses for fortune telling? What a wicked thing you have done!"

HOUSE MANAGER. *(bewildered)* My lord, this is an odd way to deal with these men. You are giving the Hebrews plenty of trouble. By the time they're done dealing with you, the hairs on their heads will be as white as snow!

JOSEPH. Go quickly and do as I have said.

(HOUSE MANAGER exits UL.)

ACT II, SCENE XII

SCENE: *On the road to Canaan, the HOUSE MANAGER, accompanied by five soldiers, catches up with the brothers as they are resting. They are lounging on the ground DL. The HOUSE MANAGER and soldiers enter from R.*

HOUSE MANAGER. Ho there, men! We will have a word with you!

(Soldiers draw their weapons.)

JUDAH. What is it? Why are your men armed?

HOUSE MANAGER. My honorable lord has sent me to ask you some questions. He wants to know why you are repaying his kindness with treachery and cruelty!

JUDAH. What do you mean? We have done nothing wrong. We honor your lord, and have shown nothing but respect for him!

HOUSE MANAGER. Don't lie to me! Why have you stolen my lord's silver drinking cup which he keeps on his very own table?

ISSACHAR. But sir, we have not stolen his cup. We would never do such a thing!

HOUSE MANAGER. But you have!

REUBEN. What in the world are you talking about? What kind of people do you think we are, that you accuse us of such a thing? Didn't we bring back the money we found in the mouth of our sacks? Why would we steal anything from your master's house? If you find his cup with any one of us, let that one die. And all the rest of us will be slaves forever to your master.

HOUSE MANAGER. Fair enough, except that only the one who stole the cup will be a slave, and the rest of you can go free.

REUBEN. Very well. You may search our sacks. Here they are. *(pointing)*

(Each man is resting beside his own sack of grain, and the HOUSE MANAGER begins searching each one beginning with the eldest. At last he comes to BENJAMIN'S sack, and the cup is found in it.)

HOUSE MANAGER. *(holding the cup high)* What have we here? *(The brothers are stunned and speechless for a moment.)*

REUBEN. *(shouting and tearing his clothing, along with his brothers)* This can't be! It is impossible! *(He stares in fear at BENJAMIN.)*

BENJAMIN. Reuben, I know nothing of this. I didn't steal the cup, and I didn't put it in the sack. I had no idea it was there!

HOUSE MANAGER. All of you, load your sacks on your donkeys and return with us to my master.

(The brothers look at one another in bewilderment.)

ACT II, SCENE XIII

SCENE: *At JOSEPH'S home, where he is sitting C. Everybody enters UR. The brothers all fall face down before JOSEPH.*

HOUSE MANAGER. We have brought the Hebrews back, my lord. The cup was found in the sack of Benjamin, the youngest.

JOSEPH. *(looking at them angrily and speaking sternly)* What were you trying to do? Didn't you know such a man as I would find who stole it?

JUDAH. What shall we say? How can we plead? How can we prove our innocence? God is punishing us for our sins. Sir, we have all returned to be your slaves, both we and he in whose sack the cup was found.

JOSEPH. No! Only the man who stole the cup shall be my slave. The rest of you can go home to your father.

JUDAH. *(stepping forward fearfully)* O sir, let me say just this to you. Be patient with me for a moment, for I know you can doom me in an instant, as though you were Pharaoh himself. You asked us if we had a father or a brother, and we said, "Yes, we have a father, an old man, and a child of his old age, a young boy. His brother is dead, and Benjamin alone is left of his mother's children, and his father loves him very much." And you said to us, "Bring him here so that I can see him." But we said to you, "The boy cannot leave his father, for his father would die." But you told us, "Don't come back here unless your youngest brother is with you." So we returned to our father and told him what you had said. And when he said, "Go back again and buy us more food," we replied, "We can't, unless you let Benjamin go with us." Then my father said, "You know that my wife had two sons, and that one of them went away and never returned-- doubtless torn to pieces by some wild animal. I have never seen him since. And if you take away Benjamin from me also, and any harm befalls him, I shall die with sorrow."   And now, if I go back to my father without the boy, our father will die, and we will be responsible for his death. Sir, I promised my father that I would take care of the boy. I told him, "If I don't bring him back to you, I shall bear the blame forever." Please sir, let me stay here as a slave instead of Benjamin, and let him return with his brothers. For how shall I return to my father if the boy is not with me? I can't bear to see what this would do to him.

JOSEPH. *(stirred deeply with emotion, shouting)* Get out, all of my servants and Egyptians! *(He waves boldly for everyone to leave him, and they exit hastily. Then JOSEPH bursts out with emotion and weeps openly.)* I am Joseph! Is my father still alive?

(JOSEPH'S brothers are struck motionless, stunned and bewildered. None of them speaks a word. There is a long pause.)

Come over here! *(He motions them to him and they slowly come closer. He speaks carefully, looking intently at them.)* I am Joseph. I am Joseph your brother who you sold into slavery! But don't be angry with yourselves for what you did to me, for God is the one who did it! He sent me here ahead of you to preserve your lives. These two years of famine will grow to seven, during which time there will be neither plowing nor harvest. God has sent me here to keep you alive, so that you will become a great nation. Yes, it was God who sent me here, not you! And He has made me counselor to Pharaoh, and manager of the entire nation, ruler of all the land of Egypt. I want you to return to my father and tell him, "Your son Joseph says, 'God has made me chief of all the land of Egypt. Come down to me right away! You shall live in the land of Goshen so that you can be near me with all your children, your grandchildren, your flocks and herds, and all that you have. I will take care of you there.'" Tell our father about all my power here in Egypt, and how everyone obeys me. And bring him to me quickly.

(The brothers all weep with joy, and embrace their brother JOSEPH, and when at last they find their tongues and are able to speak, they kneel before him and ask for his forgiveness, which he gives.)

ACT II, SCENE XIV

SCENE: *At the palace of PHARAOH. Lights come up on PHARAOH, POTIPHAR, and Pharaoh's SOLDIERS and SERVANTS. JOSEPH and all his brothers enter UR and bow before PHARAOH.*

PHARAOH. *(motioning to JOSEPH and his brothers to rise after they bow themselves to the ground before him)* Joseph, my son, I am happy for you. I have heard that your brothers have come to see you. The servants reported to me that you were weeping with joy.   How wonderful for you to have found your brothers! They are welcome to load their animals and return to Canaan, and to bring your father and all your families here to Egypt to live. I will give you the very best territory in the land of Egypt. You shall live off the fat of the land! You may take wagons from Egypt to carry your wives and little ones, and to bring your father here.

JOSEPH. Thank you, Great One! God has brought my family together, and we are reconciled. How good and how pleasant it is for brothers to dwell together in unity! *(turning to his brothers)* So, my brothers, you are to go home and return with your father and your wives and little ones. The LORD has delivered you from the famine! I will arrange for wagons and provisions to be ready for you tomorrow, and each of you shall receive new clothes for the journey. But I will see that Benjamin receives five changes of new clothes and three hundred pieces of silver! I will send my father ten donkey-loads of the good things of Egypt, and ten donkey-loads of grain and other foods to eat on the journey! You may set out at dawn the day after tomorrow, and be sure you don't quarrel along the way!

REUBEN. *(bowing before JOSEPH and PHARAOH, along with the other brothers)* Long live Pharaoh and Joseph! *(other brothers ad-lib the same and agree audibly)* Joseph, you are merciful and generous. We thank you. We will do as you said, and will return as quickly as we can.

(They bow and exit UR.)

ACT II, SCENE XV

SCENE: *At JACOB'S home in the land of Canaan. JACOB is working again at his desk with his four wives who are sewing and baking and doing household chores as before. The brothers come bursting in.*

REUBEN. *(running to his father and embracing him with joy)* Father, we're home! And we brought Simeon and Benjamin back with us, and loads of grain and other goods. We have amazing news, father. Joseph is alive! He is ruler over all the land of Egypt!

JACOB. *(listening intently and staring in disbelief, remaining stone-faced)* What, my son? *(He is bewildered.)*

JUDAH. *(eagerly)* It's true, father! Joseph is alive and he is next in power to Pharaoh! He rules all of Egypt for Pharaoh, and he has sent us home with wagons and donkeys loaded with food and gifts!

ISSACHAR. He knew who we were from the beginning, but he kept it from us and didn't tell us who he was. He is the one who accused us of being spies. He is the one who put the money at the tops of our sacks of grain. All along it was our brother Joseph, trying to learn how you and Benjamin were getting along!

JACOB. *(still stone-faced and unresponsive)* No, my son Joseph is dead. I have his coat in my trunk. It is torn and covered with blood.

NAPHTALI. *(going to his father, putting a hand on his shoulder, kneeling on one knee)* Father, *look* at me. We swear to you that Joseph is alive and he is the ruler in Egypt. It is he who tricked us, and he is the one that put Simeon in prison, so that we would return to Egypt with Benjamin.

JACOB. *(looking at BENJAMIN, and walking across stage slowly to touch him)* Benjamin my son, you are come home. The LORD be praised! How are you, my son?

BENJAMIN. I am fine, father.

JACOB. *(quietly, slowly, and earnestly)* Benjamin my son, tell me clearly. What is it your brothers are saying? Is it true what they say about Joseph?

BENJAMIN. They are speaking the truth, father. You see me standing before you, and here is Simeon. *(He motions for SIMEON to come close).* Joseph is alive and God has raised him up as assistant to Pharaoh. It is Joseph who has been given charge of the affairs of Egypt, and he administers the sale of all the grain. Because of the famine, the whole world is coming to Joseph to buy grain! God has sent him before us to save our lives! Joseph wants us to move to Egypt with our families and our flocks and all that we own so that he can provide for us during the famine. That is why he sent the wagons.

JACOB. *(looking to his wife LEAH, and motioning for her to come to his side)* Is it possible, Leah?

LEAH. I have seen the wagons and the donkeys. There are twenty donkeys filled with goods, Jacob! I believe what they say is true. Joseph is alive! Joseph is alive! *(She gives him a hug.)*

JACOB. *(falling to his knees and looking heavenward)* O God, how mighty is your hand! My son Joseph is alive! You have shown mercy to me, and you have brought my son Benjamin home. Thank you, Lord! *(He turns to his wife and children.)* It must be true! Joseph is alive! I will go and see him before I die.

(All the people bow their heads in respect and awe.)

THE END

Biography of the Author

Rolf McEwen earned a Bachelor of Science degree from the University of Puget Sound and a Master of Education degree from the University of Southern Mississippi. He studied art, music, and history in Rome and Vienna. His books include *For Love of Drama, The Good Trip Maui, Amazing World,* and *Survival Tactics for Office Workers.*

He has written plays including *The Joseph Story, Esther the Queen, The Institute, The Honeymoon, The War, and Cranking Up America.* He has created adaptations of plays including *Mad Love, Inspector Strangelove, Love Will Find a Way, The Imaginary Invalid, The Miser, Deceits of Samson, Ladies of Learning,* and *The Middle Class Gentleman.*

He has been published in magazines and journals including *Cross Currents, Beloit Poetry Journal, San Francisco Magazine, The Freeman,* and *Honolulu Magazine.* He has worked as a freelance writer and photographer for newspapers and magazines. He has directed 66 plays for the stage. He's been selected for awards including *Who's Who among College Students,* and *Who's Who among Teachers.*